A VALLEY IN
THE MIDST OF VIOLENCE

David McDuff is one of Britain's leading translators of Scandinavian and Russian literature. He has translated works of fiction by Dostoyevsky, Tolstoy and Leskov in the Penguin Classics series, two books by Bo Carpelan for Carcanet Press, and seven books for Bloodaxe: Irina Ratushinskaya's *No, I'm Not Afraid* (1986) and *Dance with a Shadow* (1992), the *Complete Poems* of Edith Södergran (1984), *Selected Poems* by Marina Tsvetayeva (1987), the Finland-Swedish anthology *Ice Around Our Lips* (1990), Tua Forsström's *Snow Leopard* (1990), and Gösta Ågren's *A Valley in the Midst of Violence: Selected Poems* (1992). His editions of the Swedish poet Karin Boye and the Finland-Swedish poet and fiction writer Mirjam Tuominen are forthcoming from Bloodaxe.

GÖSTA ÅGREN

A Valley in the Midst of Violence

SELECTED POEMS

TRANSLATED BY
David McDuff

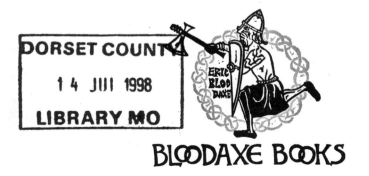

BLOODAXE BOOKS

Copyright © Gösta Ågren 1990, 1992
English translation © David McDuff 1992

ISBN: 1 85224 236 1

First published 1992 by
Bloodaxe Books Ltd,
P.O. Box 1SN,
Newcastle upon Tyne NE99 1SN.

Bloodaxe Books Ltd acknowledges
the financial assistance of Northern Arts.

ACKNOWLEDGEMENTS

Acknowledgements are due to the Arts Council
for providing a translation grant for this book.
This book is a translation of *En dal i våldet* by Gösta Ågren,
first published by Norstedts Forlag AB, Stockholm, in 1990.

Cover printing by J. Thomson Colour Printers Ltd, Glasgow.

Printed in Great Britain by Cromwell Press Ltd,
Broughton Gifford, Melksham, Wiltshire.

Contents

10   *Introduction* by DAVID McDUFF

LIFE
14   The Sowing
14   Birth
15   Life
15   Ro
16   Childhood Summer
16   And Then
17   Fourteen
17   The Battle
18   Europe
18   Night Summer
19   Stress
19   In the Year of the Black Elf
20   Incantation
20   The Goal
21   Love of the Native Place
21   To Die
22   Death's Secret
22   Circle

PEOPLE
25   R.S. Thomas
25   Copernicus
26   Stalin
26   Stroke
27   The Widow
27   Good Day
28   Grandmother
28   The Cook
29   Lumberjacks 1950
29   The Messenger
30   The Dancer
31   The Face
31   Everyday Morning
32   Everyday Evening
32   Two Birds

33   Portrait of a Victim
33   An Experience
34   Insight at Raivola
34   Leo
35   Afterwards
35   The Memory of Friends
36   Gerd Ågren

DISCOVERIES
38   Continuing
38   Victory
39   Secret
39   Politeness
40   The Motionless
40   Judgement
40   The Prisoner
41   Courage
41   Freedom
41   The Ego
42   Prehistory
42   Capitalism
42   Present
43   Magnification
43   To Suffer
43   Life and Weeping
44   To and Fro
44   In the North
44   Only When
45   Ordinary Morning
45   Nameless Poem
46   Block
46   The Children Play at War
47   Bird
47   But
48   Aphorisms

EVENTS
53   The Fifth of July
53   A Generation
54   Kurd
54   The Cry
55   Epitaph by the Shore at Vasa

55 An Ordinary Day
56 Death in Hospital
56 Traffic Accident with Fatal Outcome
57 The Flag
57 Genetic
58 Veterans of the Labour Movement
58 Finland-Swedish Note
59 The Starving Too
60 December Night

THE LIGHT, THE DARKNESS

62 The Spruce Trees
62 Spring Night
63 The Spring
63 The 20th of May
64 The 21st of May
64 Majniemi
65 The Spring at Lippjärv
65 The Brain
66 Summer 1979
66 June Night
66 Lillkobben
67 July
68 Summer Vigil
68 The Hunter
69 The Prey
69 Summer
70 Hunting Season
70 The Window
71 October
72 The Day

HISTORY

74 History
75 Who?
76 Archaic Sculpture
77 The Heretic
78 The Wanderers
78 Era
79 Life's Meaning
80 Shore
80 That Which Does Not Happen

A VALLEY IN THE MIDST OF VIOLENCE

83 The Meaning
83 Flight
84 Compulsion
84 One Day an Answer
85 Thesis
85 The Dream
85 Do Not Be Afraid
86 Action
86 Identity
87 To Be
87 Already
87 Diagnosis
88 Europe's Cathedrals
89 God
89 Here
90 Under the Stars
90 Now

A PROFESSION

92 A Profession
92 Lyric Poetry
93 In a Glade
93 To Speak
93 Life and Poetry
94 A Poet
94 Poem
94 At Last
95 Momentary Image
95 Crisis and Journey
96 Black and White

CONSOLATION

98 Planning
98 During the Speech
99 Night Note
99 65
100 By a Sickbed
100 Sorrow
101 Sonnet in Consolation
101 The Shadow
102 One Way Out

102 Afterwards
103 Rest
103 Left
104 Autumn
104 There

THE VILLAGE

106 The Village
106 The Mother
107 Waking
108 1968
108 In the Village
109 The Interment of Nestor Frilund
at Nykarleby on 14/11 1979
109 Alone
109 In Ostrobothnia
110 Memories

Introduction

Gösta Ågren, who was born in 1936, comes from one of the most active Finland-Swedish literary families. His brother Leo (1928–1984) was a gifted novelist, and another of his brothers, Erik, is a productive critic and prose-writer. His sister Inga, who died a tragic early death, was a poet in the tradition of Edith Södergran.

The Ågren family was a poor one, the father being a 'landless farmer' in an impoverished Ostrobothnian village. Ostrobothnia, which looks westward across the Gulf of Bothnia towards Sweden, is one of the centres of Finland's Swedish-speaking population – it was from here that many Finland-Swedes emigrated to Sweden and the United States in the late nineteenth and early twentieth centuries. Gösta Ågren also moved away from his native environment early in his career, and attended the University of Stockholm, where he wrote a doctoral thesis on the life and work of the Swedish poet Dan Andersson. He also studied at the Swedish Film Institute in Stockholm, and made a full-length feature film, *Ballad*, based on Leo Ågren's novel with the same title. Eventually, however, he returned to Ostrobothnia, where he settled in Lippjärv, the village in which he had spent the first seventeen years of his life.

In the spring of 1973, Gösta Ågren took the initiative in establishing the small Ostrobothnian publishing company Forfattarnas Andelslag (Writers' Cooperative), which subsequently published poetry, short stories, novels and documentary works by a wide variety of Ostrobothnian writers, including Gurli Lindén, Lolan Björkman, Anna Wilkman, Solveig Emtö, Olof Granholm, Gretel Silvander and Carita Nyström. In this way, he managed to remove some of the power from the metropolitan literary centre in Helsinki, and transferred it to a strong regional base. In polemical works such as *Hurrarna* (1974) and Ågren's own *Vår historia. En krönika om det finlandssvenska folkets öden* (Our History. A Chronicle of the Fortunes of the Finland-Swedish People, 1977), the cooperative drew attention to the cultural isolation and relative neglect suffered by Finland's Swedish-speaking minority, and added an uncomfortable stimulus to the discussion of these matters among the Finnish cultural establishment.

It is, perhaps, superfluous to note that Ågren's outlook and ideas had little in common with those of postwar Finnish intellectual and ideological orthodoxy. His far-left stance and uncompromising quasi-separatism were found embarrassing in many quarters further south and east, while the qualities of his verse were in many ways at variance with the mainstream of contemporary Finnish and Finland-Swedish poetry.

Ågren has developed an intellectually austere and laconic form of aphorism-lyric, which in its concentration and imagistic density looks both inwards to the traditions of Finland-Swedish modernism – in particular to Edith Södergran and Rabbe Enckell – and outwards to contemporary English-language poetry, especially that of the Welsh poet R.S. Thomas, who has exercised a considerable influence on Ågren's style. The presence of the Scot Hugh MacDiarmid is also felt at times. These eclectic influences and inspirations are hardly fashionable ones in present-day Finland: yet from them Ågren has derived poems of an almost steely toughness and originality, poems whose directness and level sanity of diction take them far beyond the regional context in which they were shaped and conceived.

In many ways Ågren may be seen as one of the very few still-extant inheritors of the original Finland-Swedish poetic tradition, with its metaphysical concern and internationalism of outlook. One feels that Ågren, more than Bo Carpelan or Claes Andersson, poets with whom he is sometimes compared, has assimilated that tradition into his bloodstream, so that in his writing we hear echoes not only of Mörne and Lybeck, but also of Södergran, Enckell, Björling, Parland and other poets whose reputations, during the socially-oriented 1960s and 1970s, suffered something of an eclipse. In the case of Ågren we see a reclamation and comprehension of the authentic Finland-Swedish poetic tradition, whose central attitude was expressed by Rabbe Enckell during his polemic with the 1960s radicals. Let there be no misunderstanding here: Ågren's Marxism and commitment to the left-wing cause are not in question; yet one knows instinctively that he would endorse Enckell's impassioned plea for the artist's right to a specifically artistic integrity:

> Must writers act in prisons, hospitals and places of work in the capacity of teachers, consolers and consultants? Preachers? But am I able to teach, give consultation or preach?...To communicate one's thoughts and feelings in writing in the form one is seeking and which suits one – that is what being a writer means. As for the rest, each may take up a position according to his or her ability. But on demand? I would rather be considered a reject fit only for the dustbin than act in a role I have not chosen and am not equal to.

In 1988 Ågren was given his country's most prestigious literary award, the Finlandia Prize, for his collection *Jär* (Standing Here). This is the first part of a trilogy. The second part, *Städren* (The

11

Cities) appeared in 1990. The last part, *Hid* (Coming Here) was published in 1992. Ågren has commented: 'I have been working on the three collections for nine years, since 1984. They are, in a way, autobiographical. That is why the titles are formed according to the dialect of my home region. Normally they should be *Här*, *Städerna* and *Hit*.'

This book contains all the poems which Ågren is now ready to accept from what he has called his 'pre-*Jär* era' = 'theoretically 1955-1985, but in reality only 1978-1985. I'm a late bloomer, and regard the 1978 collection *Molnsommar* (Cloud Summer) as my real starting-point as a poet.' *A Valley in the Midst of Violence* is based mainly on the collections *Cloud Summer* (*Molnsommar*, 1978), *Poems in Black and White* (*Dikter i svartvitt*, 1980), *That Which Always Is* (*Det som alltid är*, 1982), and *The Other God* (*Den andre guden*, 1985). Ågren states that 'many of the poems have been intensively reworked. They have not been ordered chronologically – I have quite simply composed a new poem collection. It contains all the important work before the *Jär* trilogy.' The poems have been grouped by Ågren in titled sections which refer to theme, and are not the titles of any existing collections.

DAVID McDUFF

LIFE

The Sowing

I do not quite remember
this poem. Everything was
not everything. The fields'
slow river drifted past
my walking father. A
yearning wing of seed
came from each sign
his hand made. The grain
was thrown into the future
in order to force it to
come. Thus was the sowing done,
thus did my father walk.

Birth

You came out of the summer into
the deep mother. You are
hysterical with life. Your screams'
radar signals seek for
echoes. The beginning's
warm, nocturnal leafy wood
was changed into the white
sand that now presses into
your eyes, but to yearn
is the only thing that helps
against yearning.

Life

Now the south wind
has come, indifferent
as silk, reckless
as love. All
who sleep in the gloom
shall be born without
mercy. And yet:
the future is stronger
than life. The crisis always
becomes breathing again. Every
despair passes
into dawn, every dove
flies home through the darkness.

Ro

I remember how I learned to read.
R and O became condensed to RO.
It was like being blinded
and going over to a deeper vision.

Ro: rest, peace, quiet.

Childhood Summer

Through the slow shadows
the cows approach, warm
evening mothers, that rather
stay than go. Their eyes
are great flowers, their bodies
are full of grass. Almost plants
they are, groping their way home
on gently walking roots.

It was summer. Summer.

And Then

And at last he came to
reality. He grew afraid
of his courage, for here
there was no possibility
of defence. He was after all
his own body. And knowledge
proved to be his own
ignorance, only clearer
and greater. It embraced
atoms and galaxies, but not
reality. All he fin-
ally found was kindness, a kind of
sojourn, and then
he stayed behind
in the dark, suffering
mass.

Fourteen

It is high summer. We play
death and love, but the days
go ever faster; the great
heart is making good headway. Soon
we will no longer be giants,
playing with dolls. We are
the dolls. We seek, but
in the darkness of the body's

cellar we find only
darkness, and in the books only
knowledge. In autumn 1950 the sojourn
ended, began the journey
through these
low years.

The Battle

The oncoming storm
of weapons, the choice
between choosing or
not, the coming landwards
with ships gilded
by fire – no, it required
not courage, only fear.
Those days, when nothing

happened, the battle was fought. Then
the shouts could not be heard, but
tight as asthma was
the silence. Courage
is to slowly
grow older.

Europe

They met, and suddenly
love was like a short-cut.
They parted. Now a veil of tears
conceals the bare kitchen,
now she is alone, in the rain
from the ticking clock,
and the plane thunders away
through the night, and the cities
drift like misty flowers
southwards.

Alas. A farewell never
ceases. Love is immortal.
Goodbye, but for ever. The
gaping blood in the paintings;
death, riding over the squares
in metal; the forests of ruins
– culture is only a face,
concealing Europe's soul,
this old, tear-filled song.

Night Summer

To save abundance
is to squander it. Like
the blazing summer
we exist, and pass away.
When that grey dust
morning fills the room
there remains of the night's darkness
only the light
from the burning lamp.

Stress

The mail falls like severed wings to the floor.
On the calendar you write down times and days.
Your life slowly becomes more important than you.

In the Year of the Black Elf

You are poor; for you lack
nothing. Everywhere there is
a stronger, inaudible place,
where hunger sates you
and your body conceals you.
Silent it is. The serpent moves
instead of whispering,
the heart waits, instead
of beating. All that one lacks
one finds there. If one lacks
death, one does not need
to die.

Incantation

Once my eyesight was
so good that I did not see
the dark. Once I went,
constant as the workings of a clock,
always towards the goal. When
I finally stopped
my footsteps continued without me
and vanished in the distance.
In the silence and darkness
I stood, free.

The Goal

Every way round is another way.
It has another goal.
Where you walk what you seek already exists.

The systems break down,
life deepens.
The goal is the road you have been following.

Love of the Native Place

It is getting light. The tree-trunks
are vanishing in the cloud-cover
of leaves. I saw a butterfly
and pretended it was
real. A hand, which I
noticed only then, let go of
me. Its deep dwelling
closed. Only he
who stays in a house
can choose to journey.
We who are homeless have
nothing to leave. Abrupt
as a cry is our life
here, where once a butterfly
was real.

To Die

To die at a great age
is no longer to die.

The old person cannot leave a life
that is already over. To die
is to continue.

It is to fall asleep one evening
as on other evenings
and sleep the night long.

Death's Secret

It is not true
that death begins after life.
When life stops
death also stops.

Circle

All is as before. The clock
draws near. Every story
must at last be told;
every answer diminishes
the question. You have moved
in your sparse constellation
of years; you have waited.
Nothing is as before, for
nothing has happened. You never
dared to receive, and your gifts
were only a protecting wall.
It is getting light; in the east
red organ music rises. My friend,
you have misunderstood everything.
Life is not the goods, it is
the price. Empty-handed you turn round,
but it does not matter. All
is as before; soon
you will be home again.

PEOPLE

R.S. Thomas

In vain he looks up
at the dead-silent hunger
that is called space; pat-
iently he contemplates
the spring's buds: they open,
sudden cries that freeze
to flowers. It is a matter of
waiting. In November
he goes over to the
window. Yes, the landscape
is visible again. The summer
was only its transient
body.

Copernicus

Someone looked for the first time
out at the emptiness, protected
only by his face. And
of his lost faith he missed
that freedom most, that
doubt had given.

Stalin

He looked around him in
the room. The silence was shrill
with suspicion. The as-
sistants passed one
by one through the shadow
from his brain. The eyes of
some turned grey from longing;
the ruler's face lured
forth the victim within them. Others
sat still as disturbed
animals; but all spoke loudly.
The one who is silent draws
attention to himself. One can
shoot a man, but not
his silence. When they went
at dawn they had none the less
to leave their silence there
and he listened
tensely.

Stroke

And the floor's darkening wave
rose towards your face. Far
away on the radio someone is opening
a fan of notes
on the piano. You lie still
with outspread arms. Your
wings need you no
longer, bird. You were only
the periscope from their darkness.
Your fall is the deep,
that has risen up
to you.

The Widow

You have gone. I wait
here, between the wallpaper's
hoarse silence, near the naked rock
of the kitchen table. Like this
I have sat long. What
I gave away is now
all that remains.

Good Day

The future is
here now. The old man sits
locked into a monotonous
shaking. There are
harmless strokes. Of them
one dies. He is ashamed.
It is really only the body
that is mad. His voice
is grey. The words cannot get out
of the mist. At last
I understand. Good day,
he greets me, and asks
how I am. The one who is
almost dumb says only
the most important of all.

Grandmother

Her spectacles are trans-
parent steel, the thin,
grey hair taut as a
pencil drawing. Does she protect
with her dignity only
her dignity? Or does
she not dare to open her clenched
fist and show the sweaty
heart? Then she dies, and
the questions stop. A heart
has fallen silent.

The Cook

She was invisible, hidden
by her shapeless body.
She spoke little, her
slow face
quiet as earth. We saw
someone watching us
through her pupils.
She was a pause
in someone else's life.

Lumberjacks 1950

They stand with deadened fists
before the camera, helpless
in the mighty jaw of
heaven and earth. Their
bodies are so used
that one feels the same
strange shame as before
the gaze of the dying man which
is no longer able to hide
him. These men themselves
never get any rest; they rest
their bodies, that part
of the soul that is visible.
I search in the picture.
The darkness of the eye-sockets
is clear, and the forest's
weight. But the hands
are waiting.

The Messenger

She was sometimes glimpsed on the out-
skirts of life; came one
grey-bright evening, went on
when the morning sun rose
through the mist and the pain.
And yet she was untouched
by her journeying. She
accompanied, she did not
travel. With kindness and
helpfulness we protected ourselves
aganst her message, or

perhaps against the desolate region
within us, for which she
lacked a message. So it was
never delivered, and nothing
can ever deliver us
from it.

The Dancer

What is
happening? She
steps into the palace
of dance, fills
the pillars, one by one,
with her body. She
examines the dance; she
glows like a lingering
flower of light on
its darkness. When everything
is finally over the dance
has been freed from
its message. Something
has been said. Slowly
her body falls silent.

The Face

His face was never
seen, for he wanted
to fit in. But
when his rest darkened
to sea, and his heart
after its last beat
finally became one with
his body, his face
came out through
his feelings as when a mountain
with its blind, stern
granite begins to tower aloft
in the vapours and clouds.
Now he is no longer
an answer to the others; now
he is unknown.

Everyday Morning

He was an ordinary
person, almost
invisible. We talked
about the weather. It was
clear that he had
nothing to hide,
but he hid it well.

Everyday Evening

He was an unusual
person, almost
visible. He clearly had
something to hide,
as he talked
openly about everything. It was
impossible to know what
secret he was hiding
by telling it.

Two Birds

The longing to be an eagle
is a crow's most typical
attribute, and the more it
exerts itself, the more
it is a crow. If it wanted
to be a crow, it would not
be one. The eagle itself is
on the other hand classical right
from the start. Birth is
not really necessary. It is only
a confirmation of his
profile. Yet both tear
at the same carcase, and share
the same fate: to be
eagle or crow.

Portrait of a Victim

The fatness is a sign of
hunger. The shrill chatter
goes with his appearance.
A beggar sells
charity; the seller
excuses his beggardom
with goods. He never
partakes of weariness,
this low conversation.
The rest of us make our hearts
drag their fetters past
our rest. But he
can only be freed.

An Experience

The feeble body shakes
under the heart's blows. Sunbeams
of blood go out into its darkness.
He waits, a condition
outside time. Far away
glimmer the years of his life, a few
misty cries, and eternity's
day. It is autumn. The grain
softens to bread, the poem
becomes words. Thus, deepened
to life, ends
every story.

Insight at Raivola

It is not love, it is
hope that saves. To
hope is perhaps weariness,
but in the desert where there is
no other coolness than death,
the shadow of the future is
all that remains.

Leo

Every step is a decision,
but still he goes. Language
stands still, empty as a wall
around him, but still
he has a few words, great
as children. From them he makes
poems, typewritten faces,
that attempt to speak. He sits
looking at his evening. A
white-hot iron wall sinks,
night falls. Life may
snap shut like a trap, but
calmly he gets up
and goes through the gloom
towards the bed's sea. Nothing
can catch the one who does not flee.

Afterwards

The need for freedom
from needs put its stamp
on our lives, but he
yearned for hunger
as a bird's nest yearns
for its body. We
hid from one another in
great mass meetings; he was
lonely as a horde of lemmings,
clear as a movement
before the tiger. We saw
that life leads straight
to death. He saw it
too, but did not stop.

The Memory of Friends

I remember the dead
without sorrow; a wood
has fallen. The gaze
has widened to space;
the waves of work
and rest beat on the rock
no longer. Life
condenses to mystery
and the course of events becomes rite,
but the message of the dead
is never delivered, for
more important than the message
is its existence. All
that was said was the only thing

that was said. Therefore it must
form the answer. Yes, death
simplifies all words
to messages. 'Good
morning.' The morning
is good.

Gerd Ågren
(A retarded child)

She looks at her body. There
is no soul that casts
this shadow. Her life
will never be reduced
to a higher meaning. Strong
as the heart she is
she brings her pulse towards the
darkness of the waiting wall.
Life is the only phase
in her life. She caresses
intensely; abandons her
hands to your body. If life is
meaningless, it must be
a gift.

DISCOVERIES

Continuing

Real flight is not to flee,
to let oneself be defeated.

Pessimism is a bed.
Optimism is a mountain
that only the desperate can climb.

To flee is to continue the struggle.

Victory

The victor has no reason
to compete. There is nothing
stronger than strength. Your
victory is only a sign
that you need it.

Secret

I beg you: do not take
your secret from me
by revealing it.
The riddle is not its answer.
The forest is not the sum
of the trees. The forest
is deep. The fields need
their water, but also
their darkness.

Politeness

Politeness is the deepest
emotion. I protect you
against me. To bow is
self-respect. When you greet
your neighbour in the street-throng
you have just recognized
yourself. Life condenses
to a ceremony. Everything
meaningless stops, cruel-
ty and kindness, hate
and love. 'Good day.'
And you part anew.

The Motionless

The motionless resembles
an intention. We can
stop a journey, but
who can stop
the one who waits?

Judgement

The winter is coldest
in summer. When
the judgement has fallen
the judge's power ends. A few
books remain
in the empty room.

The Prisoner

My crimes have been
committed, the cell locked.
I am free.

Courage

The one who lacks courage
does not dare to be afraid.
Only the one who dares
to encounter fear, dares to encounter
danger.

Fear stops then, the
extra heart in the body
that is no longer needed.

And he acts
as though he were observing
himself.

Freedom

Locked into freedom
we desperately seek
a door, but all
can be opened.

The Ego

The one who never changes
becomes another.

Prehistory

The voices are there, but
they are as yet empty.
As yet no words are needed.
As yet one has nothing
to hide.

Capitalism

Not to have is to long
for all one has not. It is
to be constantly forced to have what one lacks.

To have is fear of losing
all that one has. It is
to be constantly forced to lack what one has.

Present

To receive a gift is
to never again
receive it. To accept
is to be robbed. You
obtain an object
and lose a gift.

Magnification

It is impossible
to prolong life; let
us magnify it
with simplicity.

To Suffer

To suffer is to live
distinctly. Embarrassed
we avoid the sufferer's
gaze. The soul is visible.

Life and Weeping

To weep is
the weak's way
of living.
To live is
the strong's way
of weeping.

To and Fro

To and fro twists
the path. Thus it
has no goal, only
an intention.

In the North

What protects the earth,
so that the permafrost does not
penetrate even deeper down?
You know it. The permafrost.

Only When

No, as yet I cannot
go my way. Only
when you ask me to stay
will I have a place
to leave.

Ordinary Morning

Thousands of words peep out
in the dawn on the hall
mat. We read about
war and want, for all
that one reads remains
in the newspaper. Calmed
we drive to work
again.

Nameless Poem

Happiness cannot be used. To
realise the great moment
is to end it. A mist
of future rests over life.
Thanks to that every defeat is
a refuge and we endure
the moment of victory that never comes
but always disappears.

Block

I, who do not understand
the answer, commit it
to the darkness inside this
precise block of words.
It is after all none the less
the answer that is needed, not
the wording.

The Children Play at War

The castle's high walls
cannot shut out
the lack of enemies. Now
the knaves can no longer
manage to avoid
their soul, this vague sorrow,
and their idle
hands radiate like
useless pain.
Unprotected is the one
who lacks something
to protect himself against.

Bird

Real birds
can fly, and therefore have
no need of doing it.
They even lack wings.

But

To have attained the goal
requires tenacity.

Aphorisms

1. The truth does not require proof, only discovery.

2. Don't worry. It will never work out.

3. Let us ask our way forward, not answer ourselves away.

4. The relation between yes and no makes our conversations difficult. Are red-haired people worse than others? The question cannot be answered, for a convinced no presupposes the possibility of a yes, amounts to the result of a choice between yes and no. No is really yes. To answer no is like saying 'red-haired people are no worse than others' – which through the pointing out, the highlighting of red-haired people means that one is saying 'red-haired people are worse than others.'

5. In order to be able to lie one must be acquainted with the truth.

6. To rebel with violence is to capitulate to violence. Not to rebel with violence is also to capitulate to violence.

7. It has been said that there are things so simple that only specialists can misunderstand them. But there are also things that are so simple that all except specialists misunderstand them.

8. Some artists motivate what they do by saying that they want to entertain.
Entertainment needs no motivation.

9. Ever poorer do we go to the end of the road we have optionally excluded by choosing only it.

10. One cannot really keep watch by day.

11. Novels are truth because they are falsehood. Memoirs are falsehood because they claim to reproduce the truth.
The one who says he is telling the truth is surely lying.
The one who says he is lying cannot easily be accused of lying.
Especially not if he is lying.

12. Every love is a wall against those one does not love.

13. Every week the cultural editors defend freedom of speech, in the service of which they reject articles.

14. Fear is the soul's way of acting.

15. In intimacy there is a pain we call love.

16. To plan a poem is not possible. The plan exists deep inside the poem: exists only when the poem exists.

17. The greatest selfishness demands by means of giving.

18. At the goal the journey continues as rest.
On news of death life's joy is deepened to sorrow.
There is no dividing line.

19. The experts like Bach.
Who are the experts?
Those who like Bach.

20. Happiness is always sad, a reminder that it ceases.

21. Trust only the one who does not smile to you.
If he is hiding anything it can only be friendship.

22. Asceticism is not denial.
The ascetic considers the pleasures worthy of renunciation.
He does not deny, he acknowledges.

23. The aeroplane thunders through the night.
It is tiresome, but there is no possibility of making a move and going one's way.
The one who travels cannot go anywhere.

24. Convinced atheist:
'They believe in a life after this one. They are going to be disappointed.'

25. Everything that happens transforms everything that has happened.
For this reason history must always be rewritten – not in order to

interpret what took place in a new way, but in order to tell something altogether different.

26. What is courage?
I remember it well: to walk to the factory, in spite of having to.

27. That which is as yet without words no one can push away, but to tell is to forget.

28. If states existed there would be no need of borders.

29. Pessimism can deepen to repose, and thereby to protection against itself.

30. One does not need many words in order to demand one's right, but no one can defend injustice without a large vocabulary.

EVENTS

The Fifth of July

We no longer love
our love of the motherland.
Love is the front side
of hate. We lack
an immortal soul, and our life
is therefore worthless.
We can no longer afford
to sacrifice it. The earth
is only a blue island
in eternity. We dare
to love only the limit-
less: native place and mother-tongue,
the only place that exists
everywhere, the only language
everyone speaks.

A Generation

They do not turn round
each time nothing
happens, but their backs
are silent. The war continues
to be over. They are looking for
something, for the war
is missing in their lives, a few
years that are still waiting
to be lived. In 1939
someone looks across
the road of war at that
forest of years on the other
side, in which he slowly
disappears.

Kurd

One cannot really
execute a man.
The bandage before his eyes
goes on seeing. Gently

as sealing wings
death closes about his
body, which has always been
a waiting bird.

The Cry

The quivering stalk of the faint
cry in the night fumbles
for help. The red
darkness slowly oozes
out. For a second pain
draws in glowing phosphorous
the body's intolerably
narrow confines. She looks up
at the memory of the clouds'
drifting cities. An eagle
unfolds the mighty
sphere of wings, and rises
screaming in her darkness.

Epitaph by the Shore at Vasa

Here lie the shadows
that are cast by a few
drink-destroyed lives. Everything has
been used up, even death. Of it
there is nothing left
but to die. Their
emotions have slackened
to memories. Their
souls are one of many
intestines. Not to smile
through tears and simply
tell how one suffers
may be the only way
of doing so.

An Ordinary Day

The condemned men
stare into the rifles.
They have already been executed.
Only fear is left,
not life. For countless
starving there remains
only life.

Death in Hospital

The clock continues,
we remain
in our lives. Thus
was death formerly.

It is tougher now, an
illness among others. One
protects it. One keeps it
alive. It is as detailed
as an application
for mercy.

Traffic Accident with Fatal Outcome

Already the soul is dying, but still
the body wanders around, a
lemming horde of heartbeats
moving towards destruction. All
that has happened must die, but
every untouched triumph, all
that he never did,
this figure, aimlessly
pulsating by the edge of the road,
is now the life that death
will never reach.

The Flag

The voices from the moon crackle
like breaking ice. They speak platitudes.
Nowhere have they reached
and nothing. They have only
enlarged the earth. A flag of steel
unfolds in the imaginary wind.

Genetic

With intelligence tests
the upper class protects itself
against the people. So one must
teach the people's children
stupidity before they are tested.
It takes many years. The
clever learn it at
last, but the stupid
never.

Veterans of the Labour Movement

History is as yet
almost unused, a cry
instead of a line of thought.
We tried to say this,
but were arrested, and could
thereafter take part in the discourse
only with our silence.

Then came the war,
and the peace. Then came
the days of autumn.

We were powerless. But in 1945
of the conversation there remained
only our silence!

Finland-Swedish Note

Here and now, by the shore
of the sky and the sea,
we have to choose. Conquered
is only the one who
wants to conquer. The struggle for
the right can never
lead to victory, only
to justice. Therefore
in that struggle defeat is
always unknown. Therefore
the struggle is most deeply aimed
only at the struggle. Let us
conquer it now.

The Starving Too

The starving too can
love, but their love is
simplified to hunger, its
principle. The sated love
with help of another's
love themselves, which they
otherwise would hate. And
stronger is perhaps that
love that saves, but
deeper is the one that
seals. People, of
whom remains only
a heart and its
two arms, give one another
their hunger.

December Night

I go out onto the steps.
The southerly wind is warm
with blood. Someone has conquered.
Through the slowly
drifting incense glows
the moon's white well. Soon
the fleeing children
with their wide-open faces
will harden to strength. Soon
more people will die
in the newspaper, bloody
with printer's ink. I
look up at the ancient
yearning that is called
the future. We have
no other defence.
The earth is hot with the salt of
tears and blood, the moon is sinking
through the shadows and the hunger,
but I go in and write
this poem.

THE LIGHT,
THE DARKNESS

The Spruce Trees

Spruce trees do not
exist. The earth
is seeking with dull
pine-needle searchlights
in the opaque
light.

Spring Night

The spring is older than the autumn:
days, wide as hymns,
and nights, nights, when
only with the utmost
exertion can one prevent
the god's hazy, violet
body from penetrating
into the village. He comes

at last, while all rest,
stretched out like victims in the night,
and the silence is silent
as a bloodstain,
and someone smiles
with pain.

The Spring

Through the sparse movements
that surround the nest, the bird
stares at eternity. Its eye
is wide-open and empty. But
softly the cloudy
bird-breast sinks down,
welling like hot mist over
the blind eggs.

The 20th of May

And the leaves are loosening again
from the birches' violet
pain. Above the meadows stands
the cathedral of birdsong.
The south wind is as gentle as
a dress. There is
no defence agaist the violence
in a caress. The soil is so
undemandingly soft that the grain
has to grow.

The 21st of May

Those who fell
did not have time to die. At
Jutas they still hear
their own cries. A stone
in the middle of the flood
of days, an attempt
at order, was raised
in vain. Life

does not end, it
stops. High
above the battlefield
stands day after
day the monument
of birdsong.

Majniemi

The airless calm
of eternity in the museums
is not found here. If the room
lacks walls one will never
escape. The boundless
universe is a trap.
But here the wind moves through
the weeping birch's quivering
tears. Here the cottage still
creeps forward in its low passage
of time. Eternity has not
yet reached here, here
it remains.

The Spring at Lippjärv

The future has been planned
in detail; it is therefore
unnecessary. Straightened the road
goes through the village right over the spring.
It was done this year. What is
happening, what is happening
when springs are covered with asphalt?
Only by asking
can we avoid the answer's
hollow silence.

The Brain

A quivering tree of
birds stands over the island as
we approach. The shore's
abandoned nests are open
and blind like souls
without bodies. We bend
down carefully and
look into reality's
brain, this simple
sketch of dried grass,
where the eggs rest
and the poem ends.

Summer 1979

Over the islands in the south
hang blue clothes
of rain. Both that which
is real, and that which is
as good as real, are visible.

The thunder rumbles through
the soul, an apostolic father
on a visit to the cabin.

June Night

The motionless sea
is waiting for the rock to go.
This is not the answer
but the silence
afterwards.

Lillkobben

The sea is flowering in
the storm. The gull-chicks are
stunned by noise and
light. From a region
without shadow
they have come. Now
the sunlight thunders. The shrill

bird-cries glare. A
tern moves with
wings painfully stretched
through the light. The cries of
another are short, cold
knives of silver
against the enemy. But peacefully
the skin of silence will
heal again, and the wings
wither. The eye's islands
will be filled with sea. Protecting,
death embraces our
lives, and makes them
worth living.

July

The eyes of the tufted duck are gold
coins. Stealthily she leads the down-
chicks to the water. She
listens. The wind is a voice
without mercy. She stops. Between
gloomy, crouching mountains gleams
a lung. But every shadow
that waits is perhaps a great,
vibrating body. It is a question
of walking through the valley of death
without God. The bird's gaze is
closed metal, but does it not
begin to shimmer? The islands and
the sea, death and life,
suddenly rest softly in the
powerful, misty embrace that is
a person's tears.

Summer Vigil

A blazing lung
waits in the north. Your sleeping
face is illegible, a
message, but from whom?
We walk in the years' deepening
avenue, and eventually the gravel will
condense to darkness. Afterwards
there is no longer that gloom
of emotions, in which the human being
is shut up. Only the face
exists, unanswered as a letter.
Now the sun's cigarette is lit,
now your sleep is all the twilight
that is left.

The Hunter

He crouches. Cloudy
and grey his brain waits
for blood. Ever nearer
comes an uneasy wound
in the skin of stillness. He
condenses to a beast of prey.
The hare stops, the shot flies.
The hunter gets up,
human again. Only
the deed redeems wholly
from the deed. And yet
he is silent. The crime
can be expiated, but never
the decision.

The Prey

Life is larger in winter;
it is all that is left.

The battue goes. No one
can free himself from the chain
of footprints. Now the body is
the twilight that outwaits
your vigil. Simplified to
an emblem, distinct as a sign
of life, you will punish us
by dying.

Summer

In the midst of green leaves
one sees red, wide-
open cries. This form
of pain is called roses.

Hunting Season

Life is insufficient
as a protection. The shot flies
and the wing and its movement
are separated. But the hunter
walks home without his prey.
The birds die, even though he
shoots them. They keep
their lives. All he gets
is their dead bodies.

The Window

It is morning. The trees
rise out of the darkness, the bird-
song is dawning. The details
magnify. Soon the grass will be visible
and the clouds; we are locked in
again. Someone is opening a
poem on the darkness.

October

Prose is silent, a
landscape. Poetry
darkens to prayer.
The sun unfolds its
bleeding wings, but
sets. The moon gets caught
and lies all day
in blue glue, a grey
painkiller. The clocks
travel, an army of
ticking space-ships
through great,
immobile time. Meta-
morphosis can never be
metamorphosed. Immortal
is the one who dies, distinct
the shadow of the one unborn
in the month of October.

The Day

That morning, when he at last
woke up and rose from
the mist of his bed, the world had
cleared to heraldry.
Lions with naked faces
contemplated their souls, cloudy
with winter streets. Matter
condensed to ecstasy while

the everyday, sword of the archangel,
slowly passed through the room.
Bound in ropes of blood
an immense being sank in the west.
And night came, as night
always will come.

HISTORY

History

The summer quivered over the country road
as Eira, in dress and apron,
drove the cows from Karelia here.
She lacked shoes and the unruly beasts would have been bought
by my father, who was a cow-trader in Nykarleby Rural District
    before the war,
only with hesitation. However.
The neutralising resistance within the heavy bodies
led the cows foot by foot in the direction of Ostrobothnia.
If they shat, and they shat often, the product fell
on their knees – cows have their knees at the back;
The fact is that God made them late and when Adam
saw them he at once said 'Cuddie'.

On echoing evenings Eira milked, and the beasts grazed
on sweet meadows that belonged to others,
for this was 1944 and only cows
thought about grass.

In the dawn's soft room
the six creatures continued their way
on the roadside's carpets of food.
Never has a girl in Finland's land
had so much milk to drink!
Eira drank the Arcadian summer,
the herdswoman drank her journey's freedom
and the road's melodic peace
in litre upon litre of milk;
smooth as honey, playing like water,
still quite warm from the cows' bodies
it ran snow-white into her soul.

One day in August the landscape became a sea.
Karelia's cuddies stopped suspiciously.
They belonged to the master, a Finnish speciality.
Eira said farewell to them. Short is the way
from Arcadia's leaves to Finland's needles.

Now Eira sows the same seam in the same factory
for the same hours every day
and when morning finally dawns
at four o'clock in the afternoon
she is too tired to wake up.

But sometimes, in the chink between dinner and TV,
when the children are asleep, she hears the bell-cow's
        absent-minded bell;
she remembers the deep summer, a friendly fire,
and that sudden suffering is her only consolation.

Who?

Only slowly does the past
darken. The shadows
on the paintings condense
to earth, but the sunlight is
still there, a dull, burst
butter. The old poems, veiled
by form, resemble
filled-in forms. With the years
this poem too will vanish
into its form, and will have
to be rewritten. Every century
the sun has to be repainted. So
the journey happens. But who
is it who walks? From mer-
cy to communion, from
wisdom to revolt, and onward,
onward. Who
is it who finally
emerges?

Archaic Sculpture

This body is gentle
as a cheek. With
its soft smile the marble
figure caresses itself,
but around it
the waves are bloody with
sunrise, and soon
the face will be turned
into a grinning fist
of fear, the body's trance
be split with painful
ropes of strength. Europe
will begin, and no one
any more remember a secret,
a whispering of stone.

Man was open,
not a face. The be-
ginning surrounded him, dense
as sleep. He was not
a name, tensely listening
to the heart's pulsating
ballad. He was
the tree, that figure,
and the sea's waiting
and the sun's cry. He was
deep inside the marble
its low clock.

The Heretic

He is lonely and strong
as a burning candle
in a closed grave.
Wrapped in his ragged wings
he flies over the sorrowfully
resting heights. The sky
condenses to a smoking pyre;
under his mighty god
he goes into Occitania.

But the flight is a
prison, where his persecutors
shout down his words
with the help of his own footsteps.
He stops. Death
is only a storm. He
stops. Only now,
in the cold sack
of the death sentence, his body sealed
by fetters, does he dare
to rule. No words
any more obscure
his message.

The wood is being stacked; the fire
will brighten to song.

The Wanderers

During my childhood the unusual still
walked freely around
in their lives. Only in the 1950s
were they locked up.

Today I realise
that their craziness
saved them
from madness.

Era

In order to feel secure
people began to dress
the same, and then one saw
that they were different. Others
tried to get away. They become
so different that one noticed
the resemblance. Death
was common. Geography
dealt with hunger. Truth
seemed incredible.
If one wanted to hide it,
it was simplest
not to. Accommodation
and food were called life
in the rain and silence
of Europe's emptied villages.

Life's Meaning

The village is dying. Already
the forest stands waiting
in among the trees.
Only the mechanical movements
of a few old people
keep it away.

But every Saturday
the young people return
from their middle age
in the towns. Drunk,
muddy as shouts,
they wander around
seeking something
to seek. In the courtyard's
sea of fluttering grass
the car sits aground
while the sun sinks, in
its own clotting,
darkening blood. Here,
in the empty house,
ticked the clock, year
after year, never freed.
Here the face's warm cloud
stood over the cradle. Here
consolation awaits you, deep
as sorrow.

With hands knotted
by veins, time trans-
formed to leisure,
the old still remember
life's meaning.

Do you see the stones – remains
of one another? Once
everything was one
and meaningless. But hands
bore them from the fields.

Shore

You go. Soon the sand will be
filled with writing. You walk
in your own footprints. You are
one of your followers.
But the tide is coming in;
slowly a sigh of water
rises, welling
in across the shore.

That Which Does Not Happen

Nothing is only itself;
not defeat, that
hazy triumph; not sorrow,
which magnifies our lives;
not history, that atrocious
tale about another
future. In each event
is that which does not happen:
a silent glade in the forest
of cries, the words that never
condemned anyone to death,
the way that will
always be the way
that was not chosen.

A VALLEY
IN THE MIDST
OF VIOLENCE

The Meaning

He said: we are cells
in God's brain. The body
is only a pause, which
we must pass. And
he said: This journey
is an idea. This betrayal,
all starved violence, all
stony hunger, constitute the goal. For
the goal of a journey is not
what is attained, but all
that we leave behind. The great
civilisation we are building
is meaningless. The meaning
is that darkness we are struggl-
ing against. I did not
believe him.

Flight

They seek the certainty
and the darkness, not
knowledge. The answer is
the stone, that kills
the bird of the enigma.

Compulsion

No, no one gets away
in spring's laboratory
with its glaring lights. We
learned that. All
come into being. And myth is only
reality. The god bleeds.

But the summer grows dark
with roses. The wind increases
to longing. To be born
is perhaps atonement.
To be is perhaps
a secret. We are on
the way towards the deep, we
need knowledge, not
explanations.

One Day an Answer

At birth you were more
reality than person.
Mostly you consisted of
caresses. Your body
was one common, misty
heart for us all. But
knowledge came. The light
was no longer your eyes'
way of seeing. A bird
was no longer your way
of flying. In the end
only ignorance was
left. And you, who once
were an answer, now look
for the question.

Thesis

If definitions were possible no one would need to make them,
but every meaning ends in silence
and life and death are wings of the same bird.

The Dream

It was a strange
dream. There was no
truth, and so the lie was
not even untrue.
It was called time
and space. One imagined
walls in events.
Ticking clocks
ground to gravel
human life. It was
a curious dream.

Do Not Be Afraid

Life is harmless. Do not be afraid.
You grow long so as later to deepen.
At last life stands enframed on the chest of drawers.
It is finished. It is without end.

Action

Every victory concludes
itself. What remains is the way,
the same way again. It is
possible to learn
knowledge, to conceal that
wild, nameless bird
beneath a name. It is easy
to realise one's dreams
if one sacrifices them. And
the years, the years go by. Yet
you must act now.
More profound than all that you do
is all that you are. The most profound
is all that you must do
in order to be able to remain
who you are.

Identity

Hamlet acts mad
because he is.
By being someone
else the spy is
himself. Identity
consists in its
absence. The actor
himself is only one
of his roles. They
move from person
to person. From this is shaped,
slowly, humanity.
Right now I am writing
with this hand.

To Be

A second comes into being
by falling apart. Like
a tremor it stops
without having existed.

Already

The truth becomes ever
clearer: the journey
is your only protection
against its ending. Only
by constantly
moving on can we preserve
all that remains. Already
someone else is approaching
this poem.

Diagnosis

The traveller attempts to travel
to the horizon. And
the hunter attempts to shoot
happiness. They demand
that which is, in–
stead of that
which always is.

Europe's Cathedrals

They are the Middle Ages' vast
radio sets, tuned
to a station that without
cease transmits silence.
The message is that there is
a message, something so simple
words cannot explain. It
needs cathedrals. But
wave follows on wave; strength
grows to tiredness. Like a
wayless heath stands the 13th century's
human mass under the sky.
Now our knowledge is greater,
but also our ignorance. The
stronger reality grows,
the deeper is its shadow.
The pillars stand like yearning
waists; hymns of light
flood in through the windows.
The night falls, the eyes
are extinguished, the stars
burn.

God

God is physical. These
roads form the nerves
on his heart. Si-
lence is his outward appearance.
He plays on his organ
of human beings the scale
between fear and space.
Nothing is anything
else. In every newborn child
throbs a secret god. In
every tree a finger points
at the earth. Friend, it is only
the soul that dies. The body
is eternal.

Here

All that burns,
burns out. Your
body needs you
no longer. The heart's
steadily measured yes
softens to flickering
wind. Feeling
clears to thought,
thought is simplified to
feeling. Slowly
your room stops. Here
you will always remain.

Under the Stars

It grows dark; the
great, gleaming
brain is lit. We
are its thoughts,
an impenetrable
wall of existence
shuts us in.
Lock the door; light
a story. Freedom
is not to leave
the room; the room
is freedom.

Now

It happens that we get
an afternoon, a valley
in the midst of violence. The clock's
ticking keeps the future
at a distance. The sun
falls slowly silent in the north-
west. At last only
the night is left
of the day. At
last all that
remains of life
is still intact, for the present
is the endless pause
that we never lose, the
last, light-haloed
hour, when we
do not die.

A PROFESSION

A Profession

I look for the answers
in order to be able to reconstruct
the questions before they were closed
by their answers. How can I
put it? The work is as when
the bleeding delta of the evening
sky darkens to night.
Each line takes a long time.
The form must become so clear
that it is invisible. It is
late, the hours pass, but
at last the contents' deep
darkness is glimpsed.

Lyric Poetry

While the spring aches
in the snow like a poem
in silence, and no one
can see the fire that rages
white where the water
beats against the rock, and
the leaves, finally strong
with tiredness, manage
to loosen, and sink
into the descent, whose in-
visible pillars have always
supported them, we speak
from this body,   .
unceasingly pierced through
by spears of blood from
the heart, protected only
by its existence, and all
we can say is
this.

In a Glade

The one who simplifies his life
to art avoids it. Our
desperate scrawling on the wall
cannot conceal the wall. Yet
I write again: Here is
the source, waiting like hunger.
Here is the spruce tree's church window
on the dark. Here in the grass
dies the path's searching shadow.

To Speak

To speak is really to listen.
The actor knows it. If he does not listen
to the public's silence, that silence may
drown out every line.

Life and Poetry

To write poems
is to encroach upon
oneself, to see
if one is alive.

A Poet

The unknown poet hears
a distant blue cry. He hears
that no one is crying. Silence
is the only poem that says
everything. He writes it time
after time, always enlarged.
Unknown he soars higher
and higher. He is the bird,
prisoner of his wings.

Poem

It is not true that the poem describes an idea
as the watch-chain describes the belly.
No poem begins with an idea.
It is the idea that begins with a poem.

At Last

It is a matter of scouring away
layer upon layer of form.
When only the content remains
the poem is finished.

Momentary Image

The padding dog
embroiders its curling
hemstitch on the meadow's white
cloth, and vanishes. So
should one always go,
cautiously, as if it were a matter of
touching a brain;
clearly, as if it were a matter of
describing a journey;
calmly, as if a danger
awaited.

Crisis and Journey

Pain is nocturnal, not open
like a cry. Autumn comes.
His arms stiffen to
swords, but the hard light
from his brow is soon
extinguished. It is winter; in
the roof-edge hang the water's
gleaming roots. Slowly
a poem awakens, serious
as a smile, final
as an island.

Black and White

Reality is bloody
with content, but it lacks
form. Therefore art is
neither emotions nor i-
deas. It is structure, an
attempt to control
emotions and ideas. Yes,
form is a way of
fighting content. The
front line of our civilization
passes through slim volumes.
The *Gesamtkunstwerk* of
death and hunger in which
we live can only be
transformed by that strictness
that is called form. It is
in the black-and-white film
that the colours blaze. Form is
limitation. The artist
shuts himself in
in order to be free.

CONSOLATION

Planning

To plan the future is
to extend the present. It
stands like a spearhead
inside tomorrow's
timid clouds. No prophet
can foresee what is
already happening, and no
woman skilled in healing
will rub the future's
consoling darkness any longer on
your sores. It is better
to be cured than be consoled,
but in the end there is
no cure, and where
is then our consolation?

During the Speech

A minority of faces look
up at the speaker, scattered holes
in the emptiness. They hear of a plan,
but nothing of the goal. Then
indifference awakes and
fills the body with its space,
the brain with its twilight.
The lungs breathe a mixture
of air and silence. Life
stops being the receptacle
for empty used-up days. It
is simplified to a secret,
it is expanded to a nameless
feast before the speaker
concludes with
a final
clearing of the throat.

Night Note

When children grow up
they are no longer visible,
but they cry as before,
without understanding what it is
that they understand.

65

It is getting light. The room
fills with steel. He returns
to his face, which all
night has motionlessly waited. Then
his soul puts on its clothes:
he remembers his name. At
once the spear of the present
stands through him. Stiff,
lignified by hard work,
he got his pension yesterday.

Relieved he sinks down
and lies on in the ruins
of the night. Now it is
possible to live. At last
the future is over.

By a Sickbed

He lies complaining
about his life, a
defeat. He is still
sick with strength, crucified
on himself. He speaks
of his sharp pains,
and his waiting. Yes, he is
defeated. But one day
death rose, red
and dazzling, above
the forest of torments. We
are all forced to conquer
in the end.

Sorrow

Sorrow is our way of
remembering joy. Between
the dark trees peep the
sunlit bay's
glittering tears.

Sonnet in Consolation

Every day life becomes
one day longer. It grows
to a wave, that masses and
finally breaks in burning
foam over the beach. Real
death is not so
romantic, only one last,
lingering pulse-beat, that softens
to darkness. Nothing
breaks; it stops. All
was chaos; now all is
a landscape, motionless
as a ceremony. Deep inside
a child is playing.

The Shadow

It is shadow we seek,
rest from the light
and the darkness. We
think that we yearn
out of midwinter's dark
to summer's sun. It is
not so. We yearn
for the shadow. In the midst
of the deepest darkness
we yearn away
from the sun.

One Way Out

It is getting dark. What is there
to mourn? Love is
as brutal as hunger.
Thought cannot protect itself
against itself. It is not possible
to choose between strength and
its cruelty, between life
and its meaning. To endure
is perhaps a defeat, but
love deepens to respect
and strength cools to
solitude, and thought
finds shadow.

Afterwards

So the summer has gone.

Out there reality's back
is darkening. Cries
begin to glow in space.
The emptiness is filled
with hunger, time
with heartbeats.

Rest

The darkness has come;
every evening the sky is
a slow, burning brain
and the morning spills
bull-blood in the cosmos. Sleep
becomes cloudy silence, time
breathing. We do not speak;
we have listened long.

Left

It is dawn, the ashes
after the night. Your house
is built, your love
is dead. All that had to be said,
you have said. Your gaze
bursts and blossoms
like a flower towards death.
Anchored to the mighty
hands on the quilt
you are resting.
Nothing is left
but your words, your house
and your love.

Autumn

The day is dove-grey and
still; it is like
a soul. The bird-of-prey's talons
are weak as hands.
The autumn leaves fall
and deepen to earth.
Reconciliation is near.

There

There is a bottom
to everything. There tiredness
grows tired, and wounds
expire. There torments
grow dark, there of love
remains only
the heart, and the deed
of faith. Weakness is there
the strength that can never
fail. The future
there is robbed
of all its pain.

THE VILLAGE

The Village

The frost lay in the waterlogged
meadows like smouldering fire
all summer long. The warm
cottage protected us
against the future, but each
morning we had to go out
in it again. Each
Sunday space was filled
with thundering lead
when the churchbells
cried out to God, but
he who does not doubt
requires no faith. Each
Sunday there was a meeting.
We protected ourselves against
one another that way: by
meeting.

The Mother

Fearfully they looked at the silence
in her tautening face.
What did she demand of them? Goodness
and wisdom? The children ran
out to play. All
they could give her was
cruelty and love.

Waking

Inside his sleep he heard
the wave of footsteps coming
across the sea of the floor. Eyes looked
at his brain. The voice
fumbled like a hand. To
wake up was a way of not
replying. He looked up.
Slowly his gaze was veiled
by consciousness.

1968

In January fifteen years ago
I left Lippjärv.
Blaze was slaughtered, reality was sold.

One sentimental summer's day
I see that all is as before.
Only the tree in the yard does not look itself:
it is still standing.

In the Village

The kiln lacks both roof
and walls: neither rain
nor people can get in
any more. Two cart-wheels
are still. They will never stop
again. I remember how membranes
of whirling spokes
burst apart in flames,
whose growing weight
stopped the motion. Now the old folk
sit looking into
the spring sun to the south. Death
can no longer efface
their lives.

The Interment of Nestor Frilund
at Nykarleby on 14/11 1979

The burial re-
duces death to
a farewell. The bearers'
arms are sorrowful
as wings. The church tower's
swaying heart of
bells aches. All
that which within us is dust,
cannot grieve. A
man has been freed
from himself. We
consign to the earth
his tortured body
as gently as if we
were receiving it.

Alone

The evenings were hardest. She
sat near the window. The sky's
blazing silk died
for a long time. In the end memory is
the only pain we have left.

In Ostrobothnia

Here each town is a
footnote to the forest's
melancholy mass of text,
the horizon's teeth
are close. Here freedom shrinks
to restlessness, here compulsion grows
to peace. One travels away
in an attempt to prevent that
which must happen. One stays
here, and as the years go
life is simplified until
only earth and heaven
remain.

Memories

What has happened has for that reason
not come to an end. You must return.
Incessantly the heart beats
at its door. From this moment
to what has happened
and therefore always happens,
you must go. All that
you thought was hate
was only a wordless
document that awaits
your sorrow.

OTHER POETRY FROM FINLAND

TUA FORSSTRÖM: *Snow Leopard*
Translated from the Finland-Swedish by David McDuff
'Icy intensity...aphoristic as well as mystical...Forsström's visions
of loneliness and despair are tempered by a lyrical pluckiness...the
tenderness of snow' – ADAM THORPE, *Observer.*
Poetry Book Society Recommended Translation.

CONTEMPORARY FINNISH POETRY, *edited by Herbert Lomas*
This anthology traces the history of post-war Finnish poetry, with a
comprehensive introduction and selections by 21 poets from Eeva-
Liisa Manner (born 1921) to Satu Salminiitty (born 1959), and with
the most space and commentary given to the two major Finnish
poets, Paavo Haavikko and Pentti Saarikoski. 'This is the most
brilliant and exciting anthology I've ever read' – ANNE BORN, *Ambit.*
Poetry Book Society Translation Award.

ICE AROUND OUR LIPS, *edited by David McDuff*
This illustrated anthology has selections by the ten most important
poets in modern Finland-Swedish literature, from the *fin de siècle*
figure of Bertel Gripenberg to "separatist" poet Gösta Ågren. Bet-
ween them come mystic modernists like Edith Södergran and Rabbe
Enckell, the much celebrated living poets Bo Carpelan, Solveig von
Schoultz and Claes Andersson, and Gunnar Björling, Scandinavia's
only dadaist.

EDITH SÖDERGRAN: *Complete Poems*
Translated from the Finland-Swedish by David McDuff
When she died in poverty at 31, Edith Södergran had been dis-
missed as a mad, megalomaniac aristocrat by most of her Finnish
contemporaries. Today she is regarded as Finland's greatest modern
poet. The driving force of her visionary poetry was her struggle
against TB, from which she died in 1923.

EIRA STENBERG: *Wings of Hope and Daring: Selected Poems*
Translated from the Finnish by Herbert Lomas
Eira Stenberg writes mainly about home life, but deals with family
relationships like an exorcist casting out demons. She views the con-
flicts of marriage, divorce and motherhood with a ruthless eye, but
her poetry can also be tender and playful.

For a complete catalogue of Bloodaxe titles, please write to:
Bloodaxe Books Ltd, P.O. Box 1SN, Newcastle upon Tyne NE99 1SN.